ESCAPE ROOM PUZZLES

OCEAN REEF RAIDERS

KINGFISHER
LONDON & NEW YORK

Copyright © Macmillan Publishers International
Ltd 2023
Published in the United States by Kingfisher
120 Broadway, New York, NY 10271
Kingfisher is a division of Macmillan Children's
Books, London

ISBN 978-0-7534-7882-0

Distributed in the U.S. and Canada by Macmillan,
120 Broadway, New York, NY 10271

EU representative: Macmillan Publishers Ireland
Ltd, 1st Floor, The Liffey Trust Centre,
117-126 Sheriff Street Upper, Dublin 1, D01 YC43.

Library of Congress Cataloging-in-Publication
data has been applied for.

Written, designed and illustrated
by Dynamo Limited

Kingfisher books are available for special
promotions and premiums. For details contact:
Special Markets Department, Macmillan, 120
Broadway, New York, NY 10271.

For more information, please visit
www.kingfisherbooks.com.

Printed in China
9 8 7 6 5 4 3 2 1
1TR/0323/WKT/UG/128MA

MIX
Paper | Supporting
responsible forestry
FSC® C116313
FSC
www.fsc.org

ESCAPE ROOM PUZZLES
OCEAN REEF RAIDERS

KINGFISHER
LONDON & NEW YORK

CONTENTS

MEET THE TEAM!

Hey! I'm Kiran.

NAME: Kiran

STRENGTHS: Leader and organizer

FUN FACT: Loves extreme sports–especially rock climbing

Ethan here!

NAME: Ethan

STRENGTHS: Math and science genius

FUN FACT: Amazing memory for facts and always wins any quiz

Hello! Zane's the name.

NAME: Zane

STRENGTHS: Creative and thinks outside the box

FUN FACT: Loves art and takes his trusty sketchbook wherever he goes

Hi!

NAME: Cassia

STRENGTHS: Technology pro

FUN FACT: Queen of gadgets and invents her own apps

HELLO!

Kiran, Ethan, Zane, and Cassia are off on a school trip! This time they're setting sail on an eco expedition to help clean up a coral reef.

Just before they set off to the undersea base, Kiran discovers a newspaper clipping about the disappearance of rare sea creatures from this exact reef. It turns out they had been stolen by infamous reef raiders. Since then the raiders have all been caught . . . or so they believe—yet animals are still mysteriously disappearing.

WHAT YOU KNOW:

● Rare sea creatures from this reef are disappearing.

● This is the reef raiders' symbol.

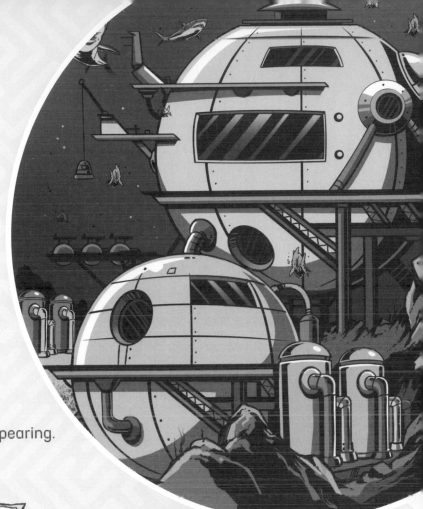

YOUR MISSION:

To tackle every task, scour every scene, and right every riddle to find the stolen sea creatures and restore the balance of the coral reef. Oh, and make sure you are back with your classmates before someone notices you're missing!

What you need to find:

Look out for markers as you work your way through the puzzles. There should be seven in total. Cassia needs to scan each of them into her tablet to solve the mystery.

ROOM ONE:
UNDERSEA LAB

It's day one aboard the undersea lab. Cassia, Ethan, Zane, and Kiran can't wait to get exploring, but first they have to sit through a long welcome presentation from one of the researchers. Ethan is struggling to pay attention—he keeps glancing over at the incredible views of the ocean.

Meanwhile Cassia is more excited by all of the high-tech equipment and gadgets in the research room next door. She's fascinated to see what the researchers use to study the endangered underwater animals. Just then, she accidentally nudges a tablet on the table behind her. Whoever it belongs to must have forgotten to set the password because the screen flickers on. It looks like some kind of tracking device, and it's hovering over a symbol carved into some rock.

Zane recognizes it right away from the newspaper clipping about the cave raiders. All four friends crowd around the tablet to take a closer look. Zane sketches the symbol while Cassia tries to figure out how the tracking device works. In no time, Cassia builds her own tracking app on her tablet. It's time to start scouring the reef for more clues.

DOCK AND DIVE

From a bit of snooping around, you work out that the research room is much deeper than the main lab. Cassia thinks it's on docking bay 4. You need to take one of the capsules down to enter the research room, but which one?

You need to find the correct route.

You did it!

You find the correct capsule to take you deeper into the ocean. It's time to work out how to get the capsule moving. Turn the page to discover your next challenge!

CAPSULE CAPERS

The gang are clambering into the correct capsule when a series of pictures appears on Cassia's tablet. One of them is the button you need to press to take you deep down to the research lab. Can you work out which of these color combinations corresponds to the capsule?

Which of these pictures matches the rings of the capsule?

The deepest area of ocean on Earth that we know about is the Mariana Trench. It gets as deep as 36,201 feet.

CHALLENGE RATING

Whoa, it worked! Let's check out what's inside.

Cracked it!

You selected the correct option. Does that mean you're off? Not so fast . . . a keypad full of symbols pops up on Cassia's screen. Looks like you need to figure that out first.

SWIPE IT

Ethan stares at the touchscreen grid, determined to figure it out. Just then Cassia's tablet beeps, and a message appears: *Follow this sequence of symbols across the keypad. You can only move up, down, left, and right but not diagonally.* **The message disappears in a flash and is replaced by five symbols. Can you swipe your way across the grid?**

 Make sure the symbols in your path follow this order.

We can't make any wrong moves.

You'll need steady hands. One wrong move and the alarms will be activated.

We only get one shot at this.

Around 70% of the Earth's surface is covered by oceans.

CHALLENGE RATING

START HERE

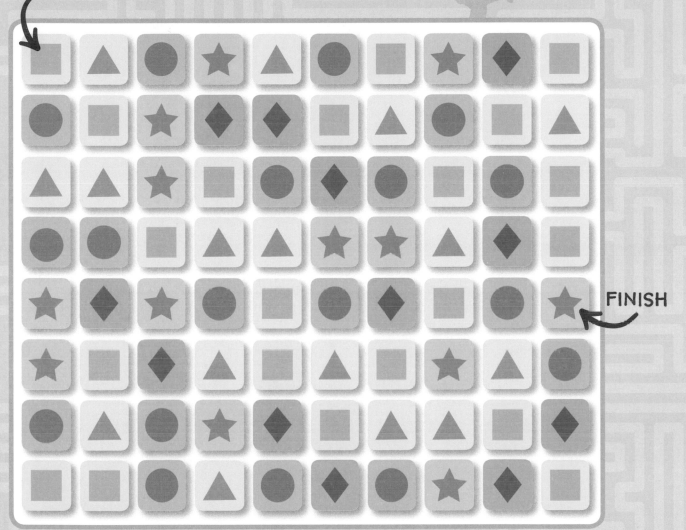

FINISH

Easy does it!

You hear the sound of bolts clicking, and the door swings open. Hooray! Into the research room you go!

ROOM TWO: THE RESEARCH ROOM

Good work! Kiran leads the way, and together you all sneak into the research room. There must be heaps of clues in here that will help solve the mystery of the disappearing marine species. Now it's just a matter of finding them. Ethan suggests that the gang splits up to start searching for clues before anyone catches you.

You're all so excited to have made it inside that nobody remembers to wedge the door open. Suddenly there's a bang, and the door slams shut, locking you all in. Well, if you can't go back the way you came, there's only one thing to do, and that's to focus on finding a way to catch those missing reef raiders.

Ethan spots a display cabinet on the wall, and it's packed with what looks like newspaper cuttings and research papers. Could these hold any vital information to help you solve the case? But first, you really need to find the light switch . . .

CABLE CHAOS

It's so dark in here, and the lights won't turn on, so there must be a loose cable somewhere. Can you figure out which cable is loose by following the tangled wires?

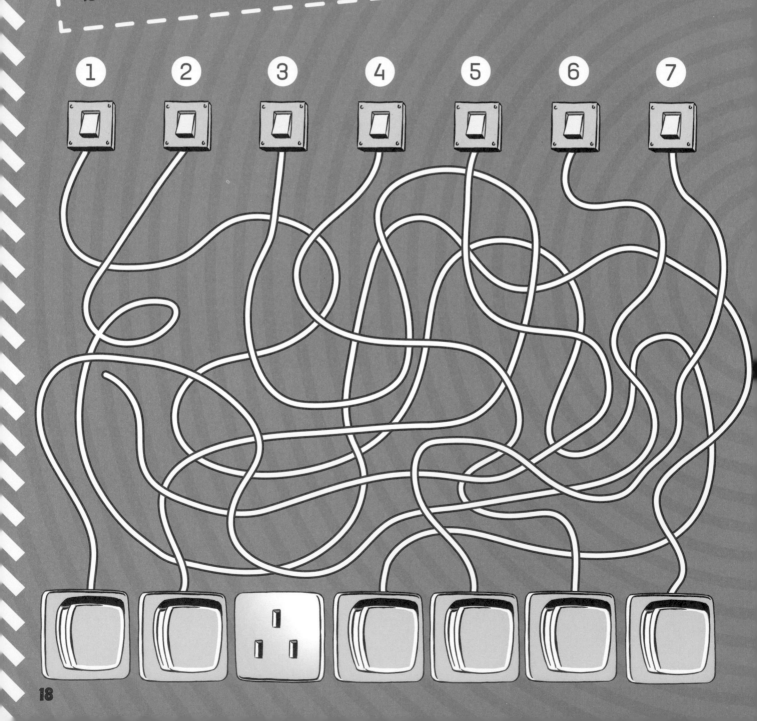

We'll figure this out. We just have to take our time.

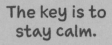

The key is to stay calm.

Ha! Ha! Ha!

What did the polite orca say?
You're whale-come.

Lights up!

With the lights fixed, you can see exactly what newspaper reports are being displayed. Maybe they will even have some clues in them.

MAKE THEM MATCH

The lights turn on, and the gang gathers round to study what's in the display unit. Zane recognizes one of the animal species in a photo. It's a giant octopus, and he'd sketched the same one when he'd spotted it from the window of the lab. Look carefully at Zane's sketch on the right and draw in the six missing elements to make it match the photograph from the clipping below.

You could add
some color too!

Hang on! I've seen
that before ...

Twinning!

You can barely see the
difference. Excellent job.
Looks like this animal is
important if it's been taped
to the wall.

21

TORN UP

Ethan hears a crunch and looks down at the floor. He's stepped on a crumpled-up ball of paper. As he tries to straighten it out, some of the paper tears off. It looks like a sketch of a mini submarine. Can you help him tape it back together?

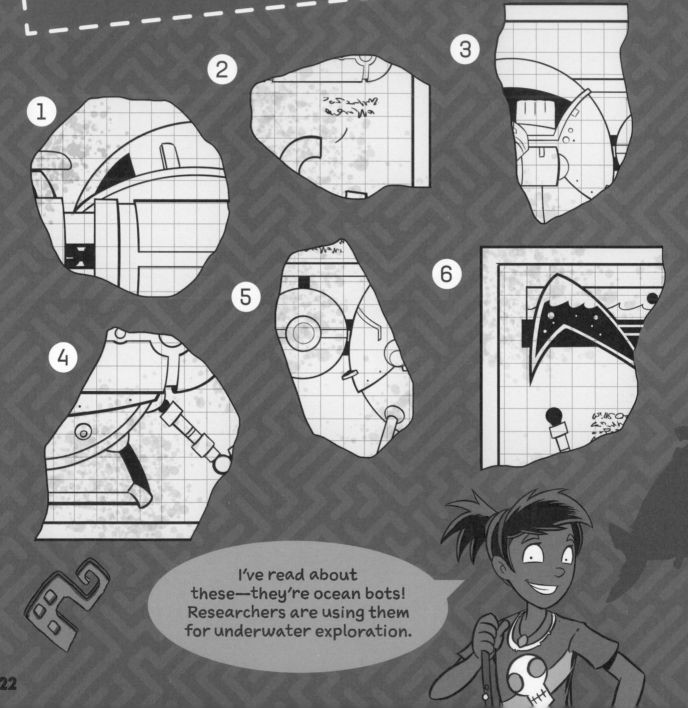

I've read about these—they're ocean bots! Researchers are using them for underwater exploration.

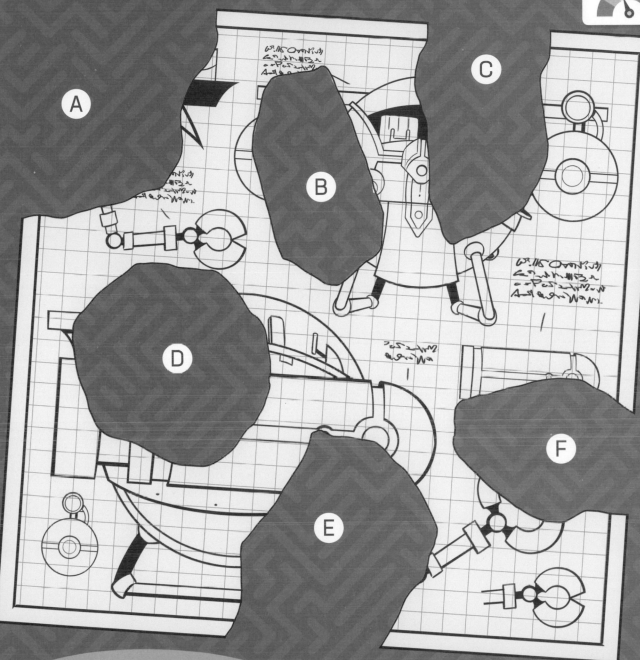

A

B

C

D

E

F

Imagine being able to try one of these out . . .

Fixed it

You spot a door leading to a corridor with loads of ocean bots. Just like the ones in the poster you've just pieced together!

OCEAN BOTS

Riding one of these ocean bots may be your best chance of getting back to your classmates (and maybe doing some searching for clues, too!) . . . but first you need to unlock them. Read the clues carefully to work out the correct combination.

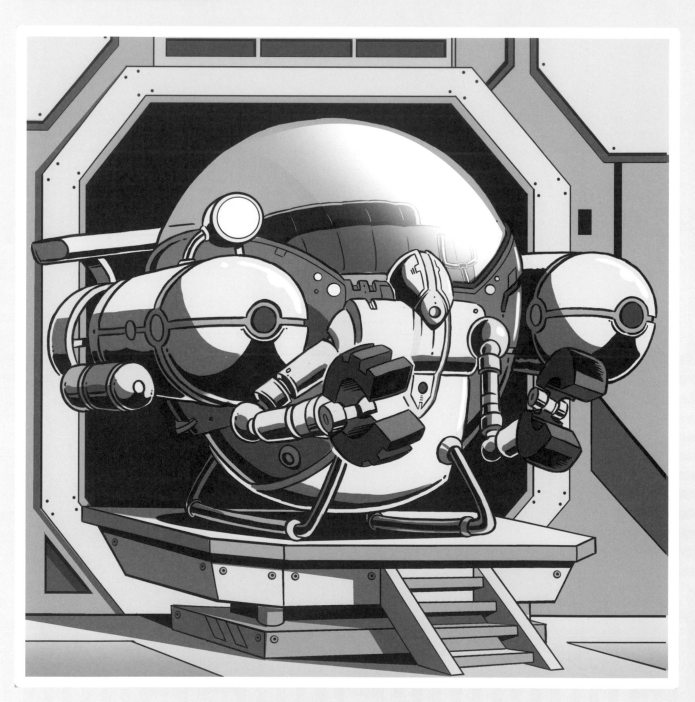

2 1 3 9   Two numbers are correct
and are in the right place.

5 1 3 6   One number is correct, but
it's in the wrong place.

4 5 1 7   No numbers are correct.

1 8 1 5   One number is correct, and
it's in the correct place.

Write the
combination here!

Numbers?
Sounds like a
task for me!

Got it!

The ocean bots are yours.
So what are you waiting
for . . . all aboard!

ROOM THREE:
THE OPEN OCEAN

Now that the team each have their own ocean bot, there's nothing stopping them!

After a couple of wobbly starts and some near misses, the gang are finally mastering their ocean bots. In no time at all, Cassia works out how to use the communication system inside the bots. So with a simple click of a button, the gang can communicate with one another—essential to make sure you stick together and stay safe when out in the ocean currents.

Ethan is nervous about being away from the rest of the class for so long, but the others are far more excited about uncovering some clues and hunting down the cave raiders—or whoever the latest thieves are! There are sea creatures out there that need your help, and it's time to save them. So buckle up . . . your mission is to get back to the rest of the class, but if you can solve the mystery of the missing sea creatures, then all the better. For now, the open ocean awaits!

SEA-QUENCES

As you're scouring the ocean, you notice rows of colorful fish and sea creatures. They seem to be arranged in patterns. Can you complete each one? Draw the correct picture to show what comes next.

1

2

3

4

5

6

I cannot wait to sketch some of these later!

On track

It's as if the rows of sequences are leading you somewhere, but where? Only one way to find out . . .

EEL DASH

You solve the sequences and find yourselves at a rocky maze entrance. Should you go in? It could be a trap, but it could also be where the missing creatures are hidden. Kiran leads the way in her ocean bot! Follow the path to find your way through the maze, but watch out for giant eels.

→ START

FINISH

Check it out!

Kiran detects another unusual symbol carved into the rock. Cassia scans it into her tablet before you go deeper into the ocean.

TANK TOP-UP

You're free from the eels, but you've all been underwater for a while. It's time to check the fuel levels. There is a limited supply, but it's important that each friend's tank is refueled fairly. Can you work out how much each tank needs to fill it up to the safe zone?

Cassia

30 —
25 —
SAFE
↓
20 — - - - - - - -
15 —
10 —
5 —

_____

Ethan

30 —
25 —
SAFE
↓
20 — - - - - - - -
15 —
10 —
5 —

_____

Phew! That was getting too close.

32

Nothing can stop us now.

Kiran

30 —
25 —
SAFE
↓
20 — - - - - - - - - - -
15 —
10 —
5 —

Zane

30 —
25 —
SAFE
↓
20 — - - - - - - - - - -
15 —
10 —
5 —

↰ Write how much fuel each friend needs in these spaces.

Ready to roll!

As soon as you're all refueled, the next challenge is to find another cave. You can see one in the distance . . .

33

OCTO TANGLE

You're heading towards the cave entrance and then . . . SQUELCH! Ethan gets caught in the legs of an enormous octopus. The rest of you must find your way to the end of this maze to reach the "tickle" button.

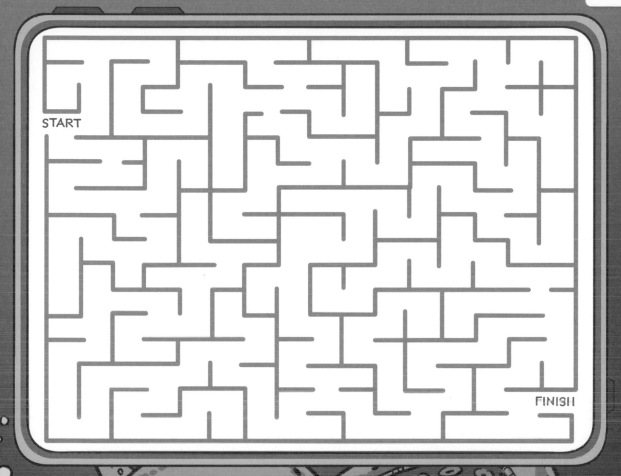

START

FINISH

Heehee!

You press the button, and your ocean bots sprout arms that tickle the octo's legs, releasing Ethan. Phew! Toward the cave you go!

CAVE ENTRANCE

Everyone starts to look for a way to enter the cave. Just then Kiran notices a drawing of a fish, and next to it are six different shaped fish scales. Find the one scale that will tessellate exactly to fill this fish without any gaps.

①  ②  ③  ④

⑥  ⑦

Yeah, and they can't overlap either!

Tessellation is when shapes are repeated without any gaps.

Now that's neat!

The gang figures out the correct scale and stands back. All of a sudden, the rocks part to reveal the opening of an enormous cave.

ROOM FOUR:
THE CAVE

You carefully drive your ocean bots right up to the cave. One by one, you pass through the entrance and begin to look around in wonder. The epic cave is filled with beautiful stalagmites and stalactites. But there's only so far you can go with your ocean bots, so it's time to tie them up securely before continuing along the path.

So, which way now? With so many dark corners, it's hard to know which way to turn. Then, in the distance Zane catches a glimpse of some glowing creatures in a pool of water. It's time to take a closer look.

GLOWING GROTTO

You enter deeper into the pitch-black cave and step carefully along a wooden walkway. On each side of the walkway are deep pools filled with glowing sea creatures, from jellyfish to glowworms. The two pools look identical, but can you spot 10 differences between them?

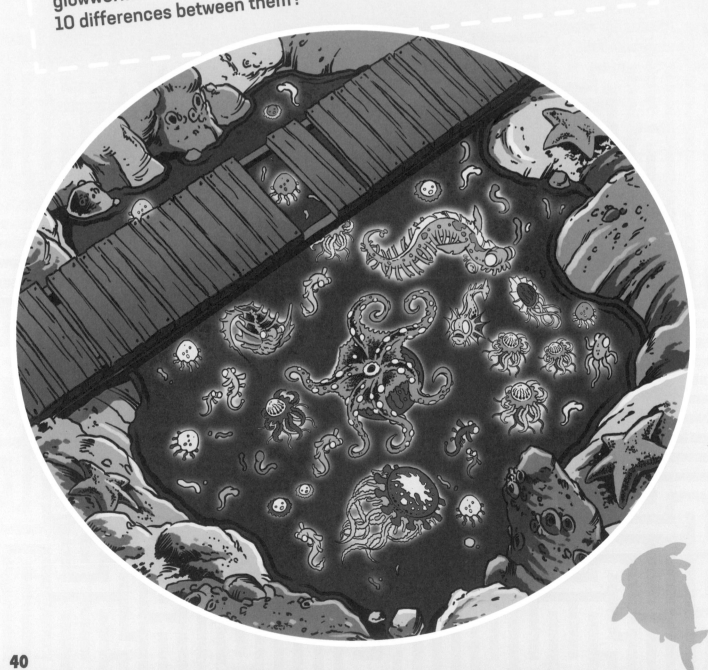

Make it count!

You've counted everything, now you just need to figure out what to do next. At the end of the walkway Ethan discovers a chest.

UNLOCK THE CHEST

On closer inspection, it's clear that the chest is locked. Who knows what clues are hidden inside! The chest is covered in symbols, and your task is to figure out the correct combination to unlock it.

To reveal the code:
- Start on the orange star.
- Go up two keys.
- Go left five keys.
- Go down two keys.
- Go right three keys.
- Go up one key.

We only get two attempts, or we get locked out.

We need steady hands for this one.

Start here

Attempt 1

Attempt 2
(if you need it)

EEEK!

That was close. You pull open
the chest to reveal another
section of a symbol.

TIME TO SLIDE

Cassia scans this next tile into her tablet, and a grid appears on the screen. Zane takes one look at the grid and works out their next task. You must shuffle the tiles around to reveal the hidden image.

These markers we found must be a clue!

_____   _____   _____

_____   _____   _____

Fill in the numbers so you know the right order to press the tiles, from top left to bottom right.

Or you could copy the markers from the grid on the opposite page into the correct squares.

Congrats!

You've revealed the cave raider symbol. Only this one has changed slightly from the original. It looks like there are still raiders working out there after all!

SUDOKU

Zane locates another cave raider symbol in the corner of the grotto. It looks like these are markers and are leading you somewhere. As you get closer, you notice a grid on the cave wall next to it. You scan it into Cassia's app to reveal a puzzle. Complete the grid by filling in the missing symbols.

The first row is already done!

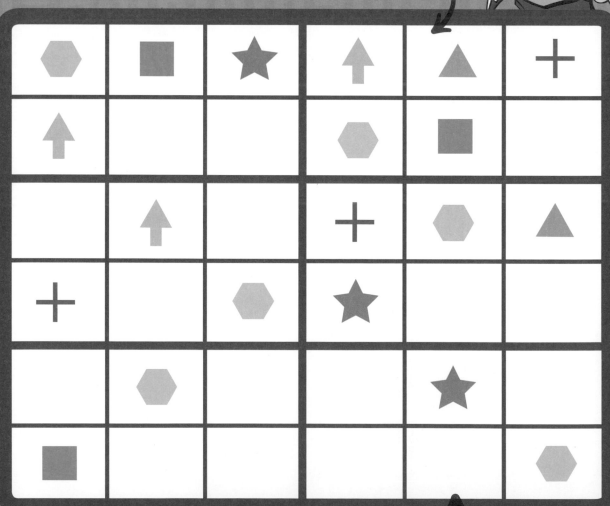

Fill in the blank boxes by writing the number of the piece that fits in the square.

46

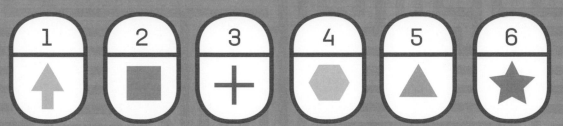

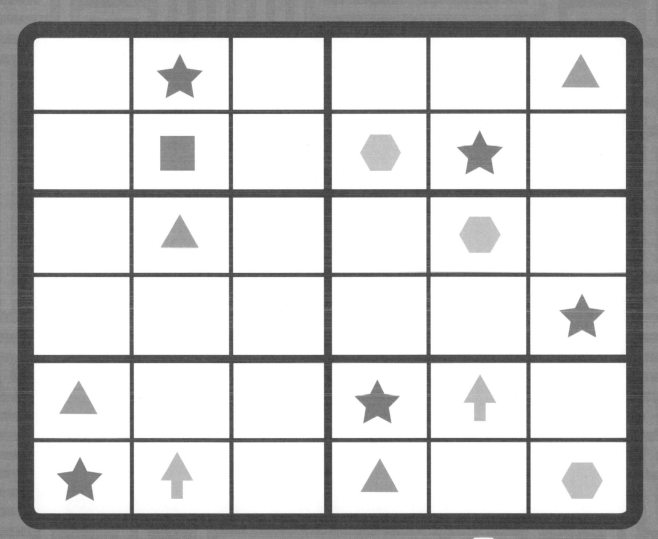

Open sesame!

You enter the final symbol, and the cave walls begin to slide apart. What will be on the other side?

ROOM FIVE:
INTO THE DEEP

The cave walls part, and Kiran leads the way into the next area of the cave. You find yourselves teetering on the edge of a very deep pool of water. You're going to need your ocean bots to explore any further!

Once everyone is aboard their bots, you set out into the deep to see what clues may be lurking in the depths below. It's getting darker and darker the further down you go. Kiran leads the way, whizzing ahead as fast as she can. You soon hit a hurdle that even the ocean bots can't save you from . . . lasers! Lots and lots of lasers.

You all stop in your tracks when Cassia's app alarm goes off—it's detecting sharks nearby. Someone must've trapped the sharks here using the lasers, to guard the stolen sea creatures. Just then, Ethan spots divers in the distance, lurking in the murky water.
Could they be the cave raiders? Make sure they don't see you until you can get a closer look.

SHARK DECEPTION

You turn up your beams on the ocean bots to see the shiver of sharks guarding a giant cage. That's where all the rare species are trapped. Don't get too close! Zane can't wait to sketch them, but notices something suspicious. Some of the sharks appear to be holograms with a mysterious symbol stamped on their snouts. You need to count the real sharks.

Epic work!

You've correctly identified the real sharks. Now it's time to get them out of your way!

SERIOUS STINGERS

With the sharks safely out of the way, everyone edges their ocean bots closer to whatever it is they were guarding. But you're all forced to stop when you come across a flurry of jellyfish. How many traps do these raiders have up their sleeves? Ethan recognizes one of these jellyfish from his book of deadly animals. Can you identify which jelly matches the one in Ethan's book?

We must avoid the ones with these markings at all costs.

1

2

3

4

5

6

Ouch

Ethan quickly looks up the jellyfish, and a warning appears on his tablet. *You'll never be safe with this jellyfish near.* Phew! It's a good thing you've figured out which jellyfish to avoid because you'll need it for your next task.

DEEP DIVE

The hordes of jellyfish are coming from a narrow waterway. To see what the jellyfish are guarding, someone needs to swim through the infested waters. Zane excitedly volunteers now you know to avoid the jellyfish with those distinctive red-and-yellow markings! Lead Zane across the pool to the other side.

START

Avoid passing any of the deadly jellyfish from the last page.

FINISH

Nice going!

Zane reaches the other side of the infested pool and finds a key. Now you just need to figure out what it's for. Zane swims back gripping tightly onto the mysterious key.

CAGE COGS

By the time Zane returns, the rest of the gang have discovered a cage. It's jam-packed with rare sea creatures. So this is what the sharks were guarding! Your task is to figure out which way to turn the cog—clockwise or counterclockwise.

Start here

This looks important.

KEY CLUES

The keypad doesn't seem to have any instructions. Kiran is sure the key Zane found must be needed to solve this puzzle, but how? Look carefully at the key to see if it helps you choose which three buttons to enter.

Hang on, look at the shape of the key.

Ha! Ha! Ha!

What did the sea say
to the beach?
Nothing, it just waved.

Enter the
code here

Gotcha!

You enter the correct code
and free the creatures. You
see the raiders desperately
trying to swim away, but they
can't swim as fast as your
ocean bots . . .

RACE TO THE TOP

The cave raiders try to escape. But just in time, Zane spots a button that activates a net. He quickly presses it, and just like that the cave raiders are captured. Meanwhile, the sea creatures swim off at full tilt. How many of each one can you spot?

You did it!

When you reach the water's surface, everyone from the sea lab is out on a boat. They are all overjoyed to see the missing sea creatures, and even more delighted when they discover that you've caught the pesky cave raiders at last. Well done!

ANSWERS

PAGES 10-11
D

PAGES 12-13
3

PAGES 14-15

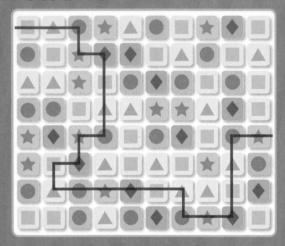

PAGES 18-19
5

PAGES 20-21

PAGES 22-23
1: D   2: F   3: C
4: E   5: B   6: A

PAGES 24-25
2 8 6 9

PAGES 28-29

PAGES 30-31

PAGES 32-33
Cassia: 5
Ethan: 10
Zane: 15
Kiran: 5

PAGES 34-35

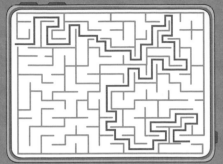

PAGES 36-37
6

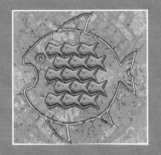

PAGES 40-41

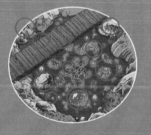

PAGES 42-43

PAGES 44-45
2, 5, 4
6, 3, 1

PAGES 46-47

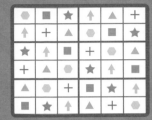

PAGES 50-51

PAGES 52-53
3

PAGES 54-55

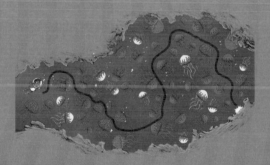

PAGES 56-57
Turn the cog counterclockwise.

PAGES 58-59
813

PAGES 60-61

24   5   34   4   7

SEE YOU ON THE NEXT ADVENTURE!

Color in the team!